EPIC FAILS
THE AGE OF
EXPLORATION:
TOTALLY GETTING LOST

EPIC FAILS

ᴛʜᴇ AGE OF
EXPLORATION:
TOTALLY GETTING LOST

ERIK SLADER ᴀɴᴅ **BEN THOMPSON**

ɪʟʟᴜꜱᴛʀᴀᴛᴇᴅ ʙʏ TIM FOLEY

Roaring Brook Press

New York

To all those who further

the Spirit of Discovery!

Text copyright © 2019 by Erik Slader and Ben Thompson
Published by Roaring Brook Press
Roaring Brook Press is a division of Holtzbrinck Publishing Holdings
Limited Partnership
175 Fifth Avenue, New York, NY 10010
mackids.com

Library of Congress Control Number: 2017957499

Hardcover ISBN: 978-1-250-15054-7
Paperback ISBN: 978-1-250-15053-0

Our books may be purchased in bulk for promotional, educational, or
business use. Please contact your local bookseller or the Macmillan
Corporate and Premium Sales Department at (800) 221-7945 ext.
5442 or by email at MacmillanSpecialMarkets@macmillan.com.

First edition, 2019
Book design by Monique Sterling
Printed in the United States of America by LSC Communications,
Harrisonburg, Virginia

Hardcover: 10 9 8 7 6 5 4 3 2 1
Paperback: 10 9 8 7 6 5 4 3 2 1

"Mistakes . . . are the portals of discovery."

—James Joyce, *Ulysses*

CONTENTS

Lost at Sea

If at first you don't succeed . . . You're not the only one. In fact, you're in pretty good company.

The Age of Exploration was an era of discovery. Fearless pioneers set sail into the unknown in search of new lands, adventure, and fortune. At a time when most of the world was still a mystery, these brave souls risked everything to glimpse what lay beyond the horizon. By land and sea, early explorers traveled to the far corners of the globe—and occasionally found themselves hopelessly lost.

On October 7, 1492, Christopher Columbus stood on the rocking deck of the *Santa María*, gazing out at uncharted waters, with all the confidence of Captain Kirk. Though he was sailing headfirst into unfamiliar territory, Columbus was certain that he'd be setting foot on Chinese land at any minute.

Unfortunately, the same could not be said of his eighty-seven crew members. They had been at sea with Columbus for twenty-nine days. That's twenty-nine days without fresh supplies. Twenty-nine days drifting in the middle of the ocean with nothing

but water as far as the eye can see in every direction.

Have you ever been on a really boring car ride? Like, your parents want to visit some park in the middle of nowhere, so you spend all day driving down the highway without anything exciting to look at or anything fun to do except listen to your dad sing a bunch of dorky songs you've heard a million times? For the crew of the *Niña*, the *Pinta*, and the *Santa María*, traveling with Columbus was kind of like that. Except, instead of eight hours in a car, they'd been at sea for *an entire month*. Oh, and there weren't any gas stations to buy snacks, so if they ate all their food, they would starve to death.

"Are we there yet?" one guy may have mumbled as he munched on a stale biscuit, looking with sad eyes at the shrinking pile of food in the ship's hold.

Throughout the Age of Exploration, the life of

3

a seafarer could be so unpleasant that English writer Samuel Johnson once said it was like being in jail, but with the added possibility of drowning. If the dangers of sea travel weren't bad enough, the awful conditions aboard the ship might make you want to take your chances in the open ocean.

The food was as terrible as it was limited. The most common food available was barrels of old salted meat and this really gross stuff called "hardtack," which was just flour and water—basically a rock made of gluten. Scurvy was a constant problem among the crew because of the lack of veggies. Bugs and rats were everywhere, and disease was rampant. Hygiene was nonexistent, and everything smelled horrible. Many people died from minor infections due to minor injuries or by getting knocked overboard while trying to rig up the sails.

The crew worked four-hour duty shifts, day

and night, and slept packed together on the floor or in hammocks in the cramped, dark, stuffy space belowdecks. Sea shanties, card games, and gallons of whiskey were all that kept them going at times.

Disobedience was answered with a whipping or time in the brig. Mutiny, if unsuccessful, was met with death.

Now, twenty-nine days into their mission, Columbus's crew members had all come to the

same conclusion—they were almost at the point of no return. These hardened sailors knew the ships were carrying about sixty day's worth of supplies, and if Columbus didn't turn back *really soon*, the crew wouldn't have enough food to get them all home alive . . .

CHAPTER 1
Vikings in America
1000–1020

"Leif set sail when he was ready; he ran into prolonged difficulties at sea, and finally came upon lands whose existence he had never suspected."

—*The Saga of Erik the Red*

*T*he first European to discover America was a Viking. A Viking named Leif Erikson, to be exact.

The Vikings were fierce and often bearded seafarers who lived in Denmark, Sweden, and Norway between AD 793 and 1066. They are, perhaps, best known today for terrorizing their European neighbors by plundering, pillaging, and burning cities to the ground. The Vikings were tough, terrifying warriors you wouldn't want to encounter in battle—on land or sea. They were well-known for their skills at sailing and navigation. They spent a good three hundred years striking fear into the hearts of anyone unfortunate enough to come within rowing distance of their awesome dragon-headed longships.

Erik the Red, in particular, is remembered as one of the toughest Vikings in all of history. Which is nothing to sneeze at.

Erik was known as "the Red" not because he'd get so mad that his face would turn crimson, but because he had really long red hair and a huge, bushy red beard. He was born in Norway

8

about 950 and spent his early years putting on armor; grabbing a huge, two-handed battle-ax; and raiding unsuspecting European villages—reducing them to charred rubble. Things went well until, in 980, Erik and his dad got into a fight with their neighbors that resulted in, as the sagas put it, "some killings." Convicted of murder, Erik and his pops were kicked out of Norway. They boarded a wooden ship and sailed west to the recently colonized Viking realm of Iceland.

Erik and his dad were pretty happy in Iceland for a while. (It's actually green and lush and not as miserable as it sounds.) Erik got married, had some kids, one of them being the intrepid Leif Erikson, bought a farm, and captured a bunch of Irish and English villagers to work as his slaves. But he still wasn't a particularly chill dude, so it wasn't long before his old life caught up to him. One day, some of Erik's slaves were working in a field when they accidentally caused a rockslide, which crushed the house of Erik's neighbor. The neighbor got mad and killed the slaves, which wasn't very smart, because Erik became furious and killed him with a sword. The dead neighbor's best friend was Hrafn the Dueler, who, as his name might suggest, challenged Erik to a duel. So Erik killed that guy, too. A few weeks after that, Erik lent some benches to a different neighbor, a guy named Thorgest. Thorgest didn't return the benches, and when Erik went over to ask him about it, Thorgest got mad. Swords were drawn, and in the ensuing fight, Erik went berserk and killed Thorgest, both of Thorgest's adult sons, and "certain other men" (whatever that means).

Naturally, Erik was exiled from Iceland for three years.

Unsure where to go next, Erik decided to sail west, toward a "bleak land

A painting depicting Vikings on a voyage across the icy waters near Greenland

of ice" that hadn't truly been explored before. Erik braved a storm, dodged ship-destroying icebergs in his wooden boat, and sailed to a mysterious new world. He spent his exile in this bleak land of ice all alone, living off the land, discovering fjords and forests and mountains, and naming pretty much everything he found after himself. Everything, that is, except the island itself. He decided to call that *Greenland*, because, in his words, "people would be more eager to go there if it had a good name."

Upon his return to Iceland, Erik the Red, a

A map from 1570, depicting the northern Atlantic, including Iceland and Greenland

man convicted of murder more than once, somehow convinced four hundred people to travel to a land covered completely in ice and build a colony at a place he named *Eriksfjord*.

Unexpectedly, Erik settled down after this, ruling over Eriksfjord as a *jarl* (a minor lord) for a few more decades without killing anyone. He had three kids—Leif, Thorvald, and Freydis. All three would go on to have adventures in North

America. From this unlikely beginning, the discovery of America began.

Erik's oldest son, Leif, went first. When Leif was just a boy, a man named Bjarni Herjolfsson came to Erik's court with an interesting tale. Bjarni had been sailing to Eriksfjord, but he had gotten lost during a storm and accidentally discovered a mysterious land far to the west. Realizing he wasn't in Greenland, Bjarni quickly turned around and found his way to Eriksfjord.

Leif's mind was blown by this story. What was this mysterious land? It didn't appear on any map. It was vast, strange, and uncharted. An awesome place for a young adventurer to make his name.

Years later, Leif Erikson bought Bjarni's boat, hired some of his crew, and grilled Bjarni for detailed information and maps about where this land might be. Then, in 1000, Leif Erikson and thirty rowers took Bjarni's ship and rowed it west into unknown, uncharted waters.

In an open-topped, multi-oared longship with snarling dragons carved into its sides, the Vikings rowed through freezing waters, intense winds, driving rain, and deadly waves. The sky was black, and storms hammered the ship, sometimes for days at a time. Many men worried about sea monsters eating them, being lost forever at

Leif Erikson may have been the first European to set eyes on North America.

sea, or even falling off the edge of the earth. But then, amazingly, after days of rowing, an incredible thing appeared on the horizon:

North America.

Leif Erikson and his crew first landed at a place we know today as Baffin Island, Canada, but Leif Erikson had a different name for it: *Helluland.* It means "Slab Land," because Leif thought it looked like a big slab of miserable nothingness. It was boring, and he didn't like it. He told his crew to get back on the ship and start rowing south. After a brief stop in another boring place, which he named *Markland*, meaning "Wood Land," because it had a bunch of trees, Leif finally landed in an area different from all the others.

It was a vast, sunny land full of forests, green meadows, golden fields of wheat, and clusters of wild grapes that could be turned into wine. Leif called this place *Vinland*, meaning "Wine Land."

He was so pleased with it that he pulled over the ship and had his men build a settlement there. They constructed turf-roofed houses and built a blacksmith shop, a lumberyard, a winery, and even a sauna. They repaired some wear-and-tear damage to their ship, relaxed in the hot springs, and spent the entire summer chilling out in their North American party pad. And when the following spring came along, the Vikings sailed back, and every man on the adventure returned home to Greenland a hero.

Unfortunately, when Leif got home, he received some bad news—Erik the Red had died while Leif was gone. Leif was now the jarl of Eriksfjord, and that meant he couldn't go on any more expeditions. So, instead, he sent his siblings, Freydis and Thorvald, to continue exploring Vinland.

Unfortunately, Freydis and Thorvald's expedition wasn't nearly as successful as their brother's.

When their expedition reached Vinland, they ran into some unexpected guests: a group of terrifying warriors they referred to as *skrellings*.

Now, *skrellings* is just the Norse word for fairies, elves, leprechauns, and basically anything else the Vikings couldn't identify. Today, we're pretty sure these skrellings weren't Dark Elves but were in fact either Beothuk or Mi'kmaq Native Americans.

Now, though a handful of men claimed to have "discovered" the Americas, before any intrepid explorers landed on its shores, *millions of people* populated the continent: hundreds of tribes of indigenous Americans. They may not have had gunpowder, steel, or marble statues of dudes in togas, but they did have agriculture, complex trade networks, and sophisticated political structures *long* before any Europeans arrived.

The Native Americans approached the Vikings

with their war paint on, wielding bows, spears, and tomahawks, and they spoke a strange language the Vikings had never heard before. The Beothuk weren't happy that these Vikings were building structures on their land, and the Vikings weren't exactly easy people to get along with, so naturally, as you might expect, a fight broke out—Native American warriors versus ferocious Vikings in a brutal life-or-death battle.

The Beothuk took the advantage, because the Vikings were unfamiliar with the land and these strange warriors. Thorvald was killed by an arrow, and when he fell, the Vikings ran for it. But Freydis refused to retreat. She pulled a bloody sword from the hand of a dead Viking warrior, pounded her chest, and ran screaming toward the attackers. Freydis was approximately eight months pregnant at the time, and the Beothuk didn't really know what to make of this. When they slowed down, the Vikings regrouped and forced them to retreat. Freydis would later go on to kill five women with an ax in an argument over grapes, so it's probably a good idea they didn't try to mess with her.

The Vikings would stay in Vinland for three more years. The first European child born in the New World was Freydis's son Snorri, who was born a few weeks after the fight. At one point, up to a hundred Vikings were living in Vinland, and they had even begun to make peace and trade with the Beothuk. Ultimately, however, the travelers decided that Vinland was too far from home and that it wasn't worth all the fight-

ing with the Beothuk. So by 1020, the Vikings packed up and returned to Greenland. No European would set foot in the New World for five hundred more years, and the land Leif discovered vanished off the maps until Columbus rediscovered it.

Interestingly, the Vikings wrote all this down in an old book they called *The Saga of the Greenlanders*. The story had been told since the 1000s, but over time, so many people forgot about the New World that eventually historians and scholars dismissed the saga as a legend—a work of fiction. In fact, nobody believed Leif's story was true until 1960, when a group of researchers found ruined Viking structures and artifacts at a place called L'Anse aux Meadows in Newfoundland, Canada. Carbon 14 testing confirmed these items had been placed there around the year 1020.

The Vikings truly had been to North America. And they'd gone there over 450 years before Columbus.

CHAPTER 2

Marco Polo and Zheng-He: Eastern Tales of Discovery

1271–1433

*"I did not write half of what I saw, for I knew
I would not be believed."*

—Marco Polo

*B*efore *Christopher Columbus sailed* the ocean blue, he was just a kid growing up in the Italian port city of Genoa, dreaming of visiting faraway lands. One day, Columbus discovered *The Travels of Marco Polo*—a fascinating book of one man's journey to China. It was the story of Marco Polo that inspired young Columbus to pursue his dreams . . .

An 18th-century depiction of Marco Polo in Tatar attire

To those in medieval Europe, China was a far and mysterious land. But that began to change in 1271, when Marco Polo joined his family on a journey across Asia. The young man from Venice was just seventeen when he left his home with his father and uncle on an adventure that would last twenty-four years! Marco and his family traded European goods for exotic treasures all along the Silk Road, a trade route populated by Arab merchants that connected Europe to Persia, India, and China.

Along the way, the Polos came across a variety of "strange" animals they had never seen before, the finest silk fabrics they'd ever encountered, colorful tapestries, a dazzling assortment of fragrant spices, and even fireworks! Most importantly, during the Polos' journey, they met Kublai Khan, the powerful ruler of the Mongol Empire, which at the time stretched across the entire continent of Asia. Kublai Khan, the grandson of Genghis Khan (who had conquered more land than Alexander the Great), had taken an interest in these curious Christian travelers from the west and invited them to Xanadu, his grand palace in Shangdu, China.

The Mongol emperor Kublai Khan

Marco spent the next seventeen years in China and, allegedly, became a trusted emissary in the court of Khan. He claimed to have joined envoys to Tibet, India, Burma, and Java. Eventually, Marco and his family decided to make the long journey back home, much to the unhappiness of Kublai Khan. He allowed them to leave on one condition: that they escort a Mongolian princess and her entourage to Persia, a treacherous two-year journey that almost cost them their lives. The Polos and the Mongolian princess were among only eighteen survivors out of over six hundred travelers who made the trip with them!

When the Polo family finally returned home to Venice in 1295, they found the city at war with the Republic of Genoa. After joining the fight, Marco Polo was captured by the Genoese and became a prisoner of war. It was then that he met his cell mate, Rustichello of Pisa. Marco told Rustichello about his incredible adventures in the Orient. In 1299, the two decided to collaborate on a chronicle of his time in China, later called *The Travels of Marco Polo*. The book became an instant bestseller, two hundred years before the invention of the printing press.

A Latin copy of *The Travels of Marco Polo*, with notes by Christopher Columbus in the margins

Despite the book's popularity, many considered Polo to be a fraud during his lifetime. It wasn't until hundreds of years later that historians were able to confirm many of the details in Marco Polo's stories.

A century later, during the Ming dynasty (after the fall of the Mongol Empire), there lived another revolutionary explorer: Zheng-He (pronounced Jung-Huh, sometimes called Cheng-Ho), who set out on a similar mission of discovery and diplomacy. Like Marco Polo, Zheng-He is another historical figure who explored farther than originally thought and who, until recently, was considered by historians to be more myth than man.

Born to a Muslim family in the Yunnan Province of China, Zheng-He was just a boy when he was captured and forced into military service in the city of Nanjing. Zheng-He quickly rose through the ranks and soon gained popularity in the royal court. He even drew admiration from the emperor. Years later, the emperor, Zhu Di, would put Zheng-He in charge of the entire imperial navy!

As fleet admiral, Zheng-He was tasked with exploring the farthest reaches of the world in search of new lands and treasure. He set sail with an armada of roughly two hundred and fifty ships, some of which were over four hundred feet long—over six times bigger than Columbus's flagship! It was the world's largest fleet until the

British Empire's Royal Navy in the seventeenth century.

Zheng-He sailed west across the Indian Ocean on seven voyages, from the South China Sea to the Horn of Africa, visiting thirty-seven Asian, Arab, and African countries. On his first journey, with sixty-two ships and 27,800 men, Zheng-He sailed to the Indian coast, Vietnam, Sri Lanka, and Thailand. He would later go on to explore the Persian Gulf, the Red Sea, and the east coast of Africa, visiting Egypt, Somalia, and Kenya. Along the way, Zheng-He met foreign dignitaries, learned about different cultures, and traded exotic goods, inventions, and ideas.

Zheng-He is believed to have died on his seventh and final voyage, while visiting Calicut in India. However, some, like author Gavin Menzies, have proposed that Zheng-He may have actually made it as far as the California coast! A recently discovered Chinese map of the world, supposedly from as far back as 1417, may indicate that

A Chinese wood-block depiction of Zheng-He's ships

Zheng-He made it to America before Columbus. If Columbus is credited with igniting the Age of Exploration, explorers like Marco Polo and Zheng-He undoubtedly laid the groundwork for him.

CHAPTER 3

Columbus Gets Lucky
1492

"For the execution of the voyage to the Indies, I did not make use of intelligence, mathematics, or maps."

—Christopher Columbus (1451–1506)

*E*ven *before he set sail* with his unhappy crew aboard the *Santa María*, Christopher Columbus was always a risk taker. As a young man, Christopher got an education and then went to sea at an early age. He married the daughter of a Portuguese admiral and inherited a collection of books from her father (which was kind of a big deal back then, in the days before Google). It was among these works that Chris discovered *The Travels of Marco Polo*. In his writings, Polo talked about how awesome and wealthy China was. Polo inspired Columbus to chart his own voyage and see for himself. There was one problem: Chris was kinda broke.

After Columbus pitched his idea to the Portuguese king, who shot him down and sent him packing, Chris went to Spain. He paid a visit to Queen Isabella and King Ferdinand V (of Spanish Inquisition fame) and asked them to financially back his expedition, with the promise of riches for the crown with compounded interest. At first, they laughed in his face. In fact, one expert at the time called Columbus's plan "impossible to any educated person." But after a costly war in Granada, Spain didn't have enough gold to pay all its returning veterans. Now in a somewhat

Columbus meets with Ferdinand and Isabella, seeking to fund his voyage.

desperate situation, Columbus's offer of a new trade route to Asia, and a vast fortune thereafter, sounded promising. The Spanish monarchy approved.

So with three ships—the *Niña*, the *Pinta*, and the *Santa María*—Columbus and his crew set sail westward toward the horizon, into the unknown. And twenty-nine days later, it became

clear they were hopelessly and utterly lost. Columbus had underestimated the size of Earth by seven thousand miles. He and his crew were approaching the point of no return, but still, Columbus was as determined as ever.

Aboard the *Santa María*, rumors circulated. Whispers of mutiny. Men saying they should just kick Columbus in the head, take over the ships, and sail back home. Yet, despite the impatient crew members sharpening their knives, Columbus seemed unfazed. With an annoyingly optimistic can-do attitude and a pretty convincing speech, Columbus persuaded his men to give him one more day.

But, according to Columbus's calculations, they should have reached their destination *weeks* before. They were lost, and everyone knew it. To make matters worse, Columbus's compass had broken and was no longer pointing to the North Star. A working compass is a pretty important thing to have when you're trying to navigate an uncharted ocean through a route that no person had ever attempted before and live to tell the tale.

They may not have had GPS, but Columbus knew Earth was round. He was *certain* of it. He didn't, however, realize that Marco Polo had recorded his notes in Arabic miles and not in Italian length measurements—a detail that completely threw off Columbus's estimation of how far China really was from his position. (Hint: The *absolute opposite side of the globe.*)

Meanwhile, aboard the *Pinta*, Captain Martin Alonso Pinzón was also losing his cool. The *Pinta* had gotten off to a rocky start when her rudder broke soon after the expedition began, and now he knew that Columbus was clearly, hopelessly lost in the middle of nowhere. Pinzón could see the *Niña* in the distance, captained by his brother. He considered signaling the other vessel to turn back and join him in a run back

Columbus's three ships: the *Niña*, the *Pinta*, and the *Santa María*

toward home. Maybe, if they were lucky, they could make it back to Spain before they starved to death. If Columbus tried to stop them, they could just throw him overboard and say they ran into some strong winds. Back then, incompetent captains "fell off their ship during a storm and were never heard from again" fairly often, and as long as nobody from the crew blabbed the truth, nobody would get hanged for mutiny.

But before Pinzón could set his plan into motion, his other brother (and first mate), Francisco, broke his concentration. Francisco was frantically pointing toward the sky, yelling for the crew to come see. The brothers ran to the starboard railing. What they saw over the horizon was an immense flock of birds. Which could mean only one thing: land!

Back on the *Santa María*, Columbus ordered his ships to change course and follow the birds.

Columbus let out a massive sigh of relief. The crew decided not to strangle their captain, and everyone just pretended that this had been the plan all along.

A few days later, on October 12, 1492, the crew made landfall in the Bahamas, and they set foot on land for the first time in over a month. Christopher Columbus, convinced he was on an island off Southeast Asia, had just discovered a whole new hemisphere—*by accident*—and didn't even realize it. He claimed this random island in the name of Spain as San Salvador.

Columbus continued his voyages from there, hoping to find India, and instead discovered Cuba.

Over the next several years, Christopher Columbus would make four voyages crisscrossing the Atlantic—eventually colonizing Haiti when the *Santa María* sank off the coast.

Columbus makes landfall in the New World

Columbus made the Spanish crown immensely rich. Unfortunately, this success was at the expense of the native peoples they encountered, whom he called "Indians"—because he thought he was in the East Indies. He wasn't.

When it came to interacting with the native islanders, Columbus was essentially the fifteenth-century equivalent of a shady used-car salesman. He traded worthless trinkets and beads for anything of potential value and stole whatever they didn't agree to trade. After all, he wasn't going to return to Spain empty-handed . . .

As it turns out, Columbus had more skeletons in his closet than a biology classroom. In 1494, Columbus had named himself governor of Hispaniola, but during his third voyage to the West Indies, Columbus was accused of tyranny, arrested, and shipped back to Spain in chains. Father Bartolomé de las Casas, a Dominican friar who immigrated to Hispaniola (the island that makes up Haiti and the Dominican Republic) in 1502 and worked tirelessly to protect the rights of the island's natives, wrote extensively about Columbus's inhuman treatment of the native Taino and Arawak peoples. Twenty-three testimonials of Columbus's barbaric actions against the native population had come to light: everything from starvation to enslavement and torture. However, despite all the mountains of evidence against him, King Ferdinand pardoned Columbus of all wrongdoing. Probably because he was a hero in Spain and had made the king a ton of money.

It wasn't until 1507 that anyone figured out that Columbus had accidentally stumbled upon a whole new supercontinent: the Americas. Ironically, because Columbus insisted for so long that he had found his way to India, the continent was named after Italian explorer and mapmaker Amerigo Vespucci. Amerigo didn't sail west until 1499, but at least *he* knew immediately that he wasn't in Asia.

For all his faults, mistakes, and transgressions, Christopher Columbus is still credited with igniting the Age of Exploration. He may not have discovered America, but (for better or worse) he opened up the world like never before.

CHAPTER 4

Ferdinand Magellan: Around the World in . . . Three Years?

1519–1522

"Unlike the mediocre, intrepid spirits seek victory over those things that seem impossible . . . to meet the shadowy future without fear, and conquer the unknown."

—Ferdinand Magellan

The fascinating story of how Ferdinand Magellan became the first man to (sort of) sail around the world begins on August 10, 1519. Magellan kissed his wife and baby son good-bye, boarded a ship, and set off in search of a northwest passage to Asia through the Americas. His white-knuckled adventures would involve mutiny, sword fights, ambushes, and death. And in the end, his quest would prove once and for all that not only was Earth round but it was also *wayyyy* bigger than most humans had originally thought.

Ferdinand Magellan was born in Sabrosa, Portugal, in 1480. At twelve years old, he traveled to Lisbon to serve in the court of the queen of Portugal, and he would take trips to the port city of Porto to hear stories of epic high-seas adventures from sailors on the docks.

Ferdinand Magellan

Magellan was nineteen when some pretty epic news came into Lisbon: Portuguese explorer Vasco da Gama had done something no one had ever done before—he'd sailed all the way from Portugal, around the southernmost tip of Africa, and landed in India! This was pretty incredible, because, even though you had to sail all the way around Africa, traveling to India, China, and the Middle East was *much* safer and *much* faster by sea than it was by land—the way Marco Polo did in the thirteenth century.

It might seem weird now, but spices were a really huge deal in Europe in the early 1500s. Back then, regular cooking spices—stuff like cinnamon, cloves, nutmeg, and especially black pepper—grew only in Asia, and people were pretty nuts about putting pepper and spices on their food. So if you wanted pepper on your fettuccine Alfredo, that could only happen if someone sailed all the way to Indonesia. As you might

45

 imagine, spices were pretty expensive, and a ton of money was to be made in the spice trade— so long as you didn't mind putting your life on the line and sailing halfway across the world to get them.

Eager to see the world and explore this amazing new sea route, Magellan joined the Portuguese navy, and in 1505, he sailed from Portugal to India as part of a fleet of royal warships. He went on some expeditions across India and even fought in naval battles against the Arabs, Indians, Malaysians, and Turks during his eight-year naval career. In 1513, he went on a mission to Morocco as part of a fifteen-thousand-man Portuguese assault team to fight against the

Moroccan king's army. The Portuguese were victorious, but Magellan took a wound in the leg that left him with a limp for the rest of his life.

The injured leg ended Magellan's naval career, but he started thinking about this whole spice thing . . . What if there was a *better way* to get to India? What if there was some way to get around the Americas and just sail straight west from Portugal directly to the Spice Islands of Indonesia?

He thought it could be done. And he was willing to put his life on the line to prove it. Brimming with confidence, a well-thought-out plan, and handfuls of maps, Magellan went to the royal court and asked King Manuel of Portugal to give him money, ships, and men to go seek a western route to Asia.

King Manuel told him no.

He asked again a few months later.

And received another no.

After the third *no*, Magellan got mad, went to Spain, and presented his plan to *that* king— which was kind of hard to do seeing as how Magellan didn't speak Spanish.

The Spanish king was like, "*Sure, why not.*" (If you recall, Spain had had some success with letting explorers sail west to claim new lands for it.) He set Magellan up with five ships and over two hundred men and told him to go claim this route for Spain.

Magellan's fleet sailed west toward the New World. It took a month to arrive in South America, where Magellan and his crew replenished their supplies at Rio de Janeiro's bay before continuing south along the coast of Brazil and Argentina. By the time they reached Port San Julian, in present-day Argentina, some of Magellan's men had had enough of Magellan's expedition. They'd been away from home for weeks, they hadn't found a passage through South America, and now they were starting to run low on food and water.

Even worse, Magellan had become *obsessed* with finding this passage, and his men started to think their captain was so determined to find the Spice Islands that he was willing to put everyone's life at risk. It didn't help that most of the men were from Spain and that their commander was from Portugal. Spain and Portugal kind of hated each other at this point in history.

Eventually, captains from three of Magellan's five-ship convoy declared a mutiny. They weren't going to take orders from Magellan anymore, and they were packing up and sailing home.

As you can imagine, Magellan got *really* mad.

In an intense battle with swords, guns, and crossbows, Ferdinand Magellan wiped out the

mutiny with extreme force. One mutinous captain was killed in the fray. Magellan beheaded another when the fighting was done. The last was left to die on a deserted island off the coast of Argentina. Men who had been part of the mutiny were whipped, chained up, and thrown into the holds of their ships.

After that, Magellan continued on, heading south until finally he found something that looked promising: a dangerous, freezing-cold passage of high winds, roiling rainstorms, and waves so ferocious they threw the ships around like toys in the bathtub.

Ferdinand called it "All Saints' Strait." Today we know it as the Strait of Magellan.

The passage was so perilous that, not long into the crossing, one of Magellan's ships, the *San Antonio*, bailed out, turned around, and sailed back home as fast as it could. Another became so damaged the crew couldn't sail any farther, and they had to be transferred to other ships. It was a difficult and terrifying journey that cost Magellan two of his ships. But after days of hard sailing, he finally emerged out the other side.

What he saw was a wide, open, quiet stretch of water reaching out to the horizon.

It was so peaceful he named this body of water the Pacific Ocean (*pacific* means "peaceful"). Which, honestly, is kind of an Epic Fail because the Pacific Ocean is actually home to volcanoes, earthquakes, tsunamis, monsoons, and typhoons. But I guess we can cut Ferdinand a break because he didn't know that just yet, and the Pacific probably looked like a vacation after having to sail through the Strait of Magellan.

Magellan sighed, his men cheered, and he told everyone that the hard part was over. They were nearly there.

What he didn't realize was that he was now about to cross the largest ocean in the entire world.

It took *three months* to cross the Pacific (remember, the Atlantic took only one month)! It was a brutal journey that cost nineteen men their lives, until finally, *finally* the crew arrived in what are now the Philippines. Magellan stopped to resupply, fix his boats, and, oh yeah, attempt to convert the native peoples to Catholicism. Unfortunately for Magellan, that didn't work out so well. One Filipino chieftain didn't like the idea of these Europeans coming to their island and trying to boss everyone around, so he told Magellan to get lost.

Magellan responded by attacking the chieftain with sixty armored soldiers carrying guns, swords, and crossbows. The Filipino chieftain, Lapu-Lapu, met him on the beach with over a thousand Filipino warriors. The battle was short, brutal, and cost Ferdinand Magellan his life. His body was never recovered.

Well, this story just took an interesting turn, didn't it?

The expedition, now down to only two ships, still needed to get home. The crews appointed two men—one Portuguese, and one Spanish—to lead them, but those men were killed four days later when a *different* Filipino tribe invited them over for dinner and then attacked them while they were eating their appetizers. Another guy, João Lopes de Carvalho, took over from there, but he got lost in the Philippines and ended up sailing around aimlessly for six months before finally getting them to the Spice

Islands—a trip that should have taken only a few days.

Circulus Aequinoctialis.

Prima ego velivolis ambivi cursibus Orbem,
Magellane novo te duce ducta freto.
Ambivi, meritoq; vocor VICTORIA: sunt mi
Vela, alæ; precium, gloria; pugna, mare.

Magellan's ship *Victoria*, as depicted on a 1590 map by Ortelius

The expedition loaded up on rare spices in the Spice Islands. Before they set sail for home, the crew elected a new commander—a Spaniard named Juan Sebastian Elcano. Elcano was just a regular sailor who had participated in the mutiny against Magellan (and had been locked up in chains in the ship's dungeon for *five months* of the trip!), but after proving himself a leader, he became the captain of the *Victoria*. And, luckily, this was a guy who clearly knew what he was doing. Elcano took command and ordered his men to strip apart one of the damaged ships so they could use the parts to repair the other one. Finally, in November 1521, Elcano left the Spice Islands to begin the long ride back to Spain.

It took almost a year.

By the time Elcano arrived back in Spain, they had covered roughly 50,500 miles across the world. Of the five ships and 270 men that had departed, just eighteen men returned alive, aboard one smashed-up, falling-apart ship that they managed to fill with some of the most valuable spices and goods in the world. Elcano was given a coat of arms and a yearly pension. He became an instant hero in Spain. He had finished the first circumnavigation (the word for sailing around the world in a circle) in human history. The route itself was so unbelievably difficult that it wasn't attempted again for almost sixty more years, but the expedition did wonders to expand human knowledge of our planet. It proved definitively that Earth was round (most people knew that, but the Church was still a little cranky about it), that it could be sailed around in a circle, and that it was far bigger than anyone could have possibly imagined.

CHAPTER 5
The "Failure" of Giovanni da Verrazzano

1524

"A new land, never before seen by ancient or modern eye . . ."

—Giovanni da Verrazzano (1485–1528)

In a short period of time, the New World, which had started out as "that one giant unexplored landmass thingy between Europe and Asia," started to take shape. European pioneers began to painstakingly map North and South America, piece by piece, like a puzzle. One of the first explorers to map the eastern coast of North America was Giovanni da Verrazzano.

Born in Italy in 1485, Giovanni was always curious about the world beyond his village. Growing up, he studied as many books and maps as he could get his hands on. He was inspired by the likes of Amerigo Vespucci (the guy whom America is named after), Ponce de Leon (the Spanish explorer who discovered Florida), and Vasco da Gama (the first European to sail to India around Africa), but it was Portuguese explorer Ferdinand Magellan who persuaded him to pursue his endeavor of discovery. Like Magellan, Giovanni hoped to either find a westward route to Asia, around America—what would come to be known as the Northwest Passage—or strike it rich in the New World. Together with his brother and navigator, Gerolamo, Verrazzano made his way to France in 1523.

King Francis I hired Giovanni and Gerolamo to claim a piece of the New World for France. Giovanni and his brother had requested four

Giovanni da Verrazzano

ships, but Francis gave them only one. He also provided them with only five percent of the money they needed to actually fund the expedition work, but hey, it was a start. Luckily, they knew a few friends with rich relatives and managed to raise enough capital through some old-school fund-raising, eventually assembling a fleet of four ships under Giovanni's command.

After gathering the money, crew, ships, and food, the Verrazzano brothers were ready to set sail. But then another problem quickly reared its head—the French declared war against Portugal. So now, instead of just discovering uncharted lands in dangerous waters, the Verrazzano brothers also had to wait for the right moment to sneak out of the Mediterranean Sea and around the Portuguese navy, without getting conscripted or blown up into driftwood.

Aboard his flagship, the *Dauphine*, Giovanni led his four vessels past the navy and into the Atlantic in the middle of winter. Almost immediately, they were struck by severe storms, which forced them to head for shore in England. Two of the ships sank en route, but the Verrazzanos were unfazed. After repairs to the *Dauphine* and the *Normanda*, the Super Verrazzano Bros. once again set off for the New World.

Unfortunately, right before they left port, news arrived that France was also at war with Spain. Because of this, the *Normanda* was recalled back into military service, leaving Giovanni and his brother with just one little ship: the *Dauphine* and fifty French sailors. Just to recap, they started out with one ship, gained three more, and then lost three, leaving them once again with one ship. Maybe it was just meant to be?

The brothers *finally* got under way on January 17, 1524. Then on February 24, the crew was greeted with another surprise gale that threatened to capsize them. "Really?!" Giovanni probably muttered under his breath, soaking wet on the windswept deck as the thunder bellowed overhead. This time, however, Giovanni and Gerolamo triumphed over the stormy seas. One month later, they arrived at Cape Fear, North Carolina. Of course, back then it wasn't called that. From there, Giovanni sailed north, up the East Coast in search of the fabled

(and nonexistent) Northwest Passage to the Pacific Ocean. Throughout the journey, Giovanni wrote detailed logs about their adventures, while his brother mapped their course. If you look at them today, you can see that Gerolamo's maps were insanely accurate for their time.

As the brothers looked for a good spot along the coast to drop anchor, they saw a great fire on the shore—a man-made fire. They could see a tribe of Native Americans on the beach staring back at them in wonder. But as the ship got

closer, they began running for the woods, occasionally popping up from behind the bushes to watch the ship. The crew were wary of stopping, but Giovanni was determined to say hi.

Giovanni da Verrazzano was the first to come ashore. Soaking wet, in a floppy hat, he waded through the waves and stepped onto the beach with his hands stretched out in a nonthreatening fashion. Slowly and cautiously, the indigenous people came out to get a closer look. They walked up to him and immediately started touching his clothes and grabbing his beard in a curious but friendly manner (the men of this particular tribe couldn't really grow huge, awesome beards).

Eventually, the rest of the crew warmed up to the natives, and they became friendly. Everyone was having so much fun, in fact, that they had already waved good-bye and sailed on when the crew realized they'd forgotten to fill up their water flasks. A few days later, their water supply was so low they looked for a spot to go ashore again. Luckily, they spotted another tribe of Native Americans, the Lenape, who seemed genuinely happy to see them. Giovanni hoped they could trade goods with the Lenape for some H_2O.

The waves were too rough to send a longboat out, so they sent their best swimmer with a bag of cool stuff to trade: mirrors, bells, that sort of thing. On his way back over to the ship, the waves picked up, knocking him around like a tennis ball before throwing him back onto the beach, battered, soaking wet, and unconscious.

At first, Giovanni was worried the young sailor was dead. That's when he saw the Lenape approach their man on the beach. Just as the natives lifted the young man and began to carry him farther from the shore, he woke and began to cry out in fear. The crew could do nothing but watch in disbelief from the ship as they carried him away kicking and screaming toward a large fire. They laid him down beside the fire and stripped him of his wet clothes. Aboard the ship, Giovanni and his crew feared the worst.

Turns out, though, that the Lenape were liter-ally just trying to dry him off. After an awkward game of charades, the sailor explained that he needed to head back to the ship. However, the natives wouldn't let him leave . . . without first giving a hug. Giovanni let out a long sigh of relief.

The explorers continued on, past Virginia, Maryland, Delaware, and New Jersey, eventually discovering the entrance to a huge river we know today as the Hudson (named after British explorer Henry Hudson, who discovered the river and later went missing in the Arctic Circle after his crew mutinied against him). On July 8,

1524, the Verrazzano brothers returned to France after their six-month journey. Despite their success in mapping two thousand miles of undiscovered coastline, the French king was not pleased. They'd ultimately failed in their mission to find a new route to Asia.

In 1528, Giovanni da Verrazzano set out on one final voyage—this time to South America, where he stopped at the island of Guadeloupe. Moments after his arrival, he was savagely attacked by a tribe of cannibals, killed, and turned into a main course as his brother watched helplessly from the ship.

Giovanni never found a northern route to the Pacific. During his time, Giovanni da Verrazzano may have been regarded as an Epic Failure, but the history books remember him as one of the most courageous and important figures of the Age of Exploration. Despite his untimely

French explorer Samuel de Champlain is welcomed by the Iroquoians in Québec. Many French explorers in Canada had good relations with the native peoples.

demise, many of the French explorers that came after Giovanni, like Jacques Cartier and Samuel de Champlain, followed Verrazzano's example of having good relations with native peoples they encountered during their exploration of Canada. Today the Verrazano-Narrows Bridge in New York is named (though inaccurately spelled) in his honor.

CHAPTER 6
Cabeza de Vaca: Castaway in Mexico
1527–1536

"One-third of our people were dangerously ill, getting worse hourly, and we felt sure of meeting the same fate, with death as our only prospect . . ."

—Cabeza de Vaca

On June 17, 1527, a Spanish fleet of five ships with a crew of six hundred set sail for Florida.

In *April 1536*—almost nine years after their departure—the last four survivors of the disastrous expedition were discovered wandering around Mexico. This legendary journey, recorded by Álvar Núñez Cabeza de Vaca, is a perfect example of Murphy's Law: Anything that can go wrong, will.

In 1527, King Charles I of Spain chose Spanish conquistador Governor Pánfilo de Narváez to lead an expedition to Florida, to pick up where the famed Ponce de Leon had left off by establishing a permanent colony in the name of Spain. He was given permission to settle all the land between Rio de las Palmas (in modern-day Mexico) and Florida: basically, the entire Gulf of Mexico region. Many Spanish nobles joined him with dreams of wealth and power—among them Andres Dorantes, Alonso del Castillo Maldonado, and Álvar Núñez Cabeza de Vaca.

Cabeza de Vaca was the expedition's royal treasurer. He came from a military background (his grandfather was a famous conquistador), and he decided to continue the family business. Cabeza de Vaca, Dorantes, and Castillo set sail

Cabeza de Vaca

for Florida in search of glory, but their voyage was cursed from the moment they departed.

The journey across the Atlantic Ocean was long and grueling. Not only were the travelers cramped together with tons of smelly farm animals (they would need them for farming once their colony was established), but they also had barely enough to eat and were getting tossed around belowdecks like they were in a wooden washing machine. This monthlong journey was so unpleasant that after arriving in Hispaniola for supplies, 140 crew members decided they'd had enough sailing for one lifetime and stayed behind in the Caribbean. Little did they know they were 140 of the  luckiest deserters ever.

What remained of the crew sailed to Cuba, where they picked up more supplies for their expedition. That's when it started to rain. And then the weather got worse. Like, way worse.

The wind howled, and thunder cracked. As the sails of Cabeza de Vaca's ship threatened to blow away, a messenger urged the treasurer to come ashore to oversee the transfer of goods. Cabeza de Vaca refused, not wanting to leave his ship behind with the storm picking up, but the messenger eventually convinced him. When Cabeza de Vaca got to shore, they got hit by a full-blown hurricane.

You see, back in the day, there was no meteorologist to predict things like hurricanes and fierce thunderstorms, so sailors just had to hope for the best. Cabeza de Vaca and the others had seen bad storms before, but none had ever experienced anything quite like this. Huge trees were thrown like footballs, and houses collapsed as if they were made of toothpicks. The Spaniards huddled together and tried to find shelter. The native Tainos called it *hurakan*, meaning "big wind," but Cabeza de Vaca saw it as a terrible omen of things to come.

The next morning, after the wind had died down, the shaken survivors made their way to the shore to find that both of their ships were missing and that they'd lost sixty good men to the storm. A mile down the beach, they found a rowboat stuck in a tree. As stubborn as Narváez was, even he had to admit this was a bit of a setback. They postponed their voyage for a year while they did their best to replace their ships, their crew, and their horses.

Cabeza de Vaca and others were starting to have second thoughts, but Narváez was still determined to make something out of his miserable time in the New World. However, Florida was no longer his primary goal. Narváez changed direction when he heard rumors that riches were flowing from Rio de las Palmas, Mexico, and he wanted to be the first to claim all that sweet treasure for himself.

This new course meant they would need to find a new navigator. Someone who knew the region. They found a man by the name of Diego Miruelo to pilot the fleet. Unfortunately, they didn't realize that Miruelo had no idea where

 he was going or that he knew even less about piloting a ship. He was as overconfident as he was incompetent and inexperienced.

Miruelo managed to run the ships aground on multiple occasions before they even left Cuba. To make matters worse, they ran into not one, not two, but *three* more increasingly violent storms. Only forty-two of their eighty horses survived the trip. The crew was in bad shape.

Thanks to Miruelo's "skill," when they finally spotted land on April 12, 1528, they weren't just nine hundred miles off course, they were on the wrong side of the Gulf of Mexico—off the coast of Florida. Tampa Bay, to be exact. Regardless, Narváez assumed that they were on the right track, after Miruelo convinced him that Rio de las Palmas was no more than thirty miles north.

It wasn't.

Cabeza de Vaca wasn't an idiot, and he voiced his concerns, but Captain Narváez was undeterred. He planned to head up the coast by foot to their destination. Instead of turning

back, Cabeza de Vaca and about three hundred soldiers decided to follow Narváez on his suicide mission, stumbling aimlessly into the depths of Florida. Everyone else said "No thanks," got back on the ships, and sailed away. Nobody ever saw them again.

After about four months of trudging through swampland, fending off native tribes who saw them as trespassers, and getting hopelessly lost, the remaining 250 Spaniards realized they'd made a terrible mistake. They set up camp at Apalachee Bay, hoping for a search party, but rescue never came.

After being forced to eat their horses to avoid starvation, the castaway crew planned one last-ditch effort to make it across the Gulf of Mexico. They melted their guns down into tools and nails and got to work. Together they managed to build five makeshift rafts out of logs and (I kid you not) horsehair, sewing their shirts together as sails. MacGyver would have been proud.

Between September and November, the make-shift flotilla made its way west along the Gulf Coast, past what is now Alabama, Mississippi, and Louisiana, sailing over 750 miles. They were all slowly dying of thirst when they were mirac-ulously saved by the fresh water at the mouth of the Mississippi River. Unfortunately, the force of the Mississippi pushed them farther out to sea, where they all soon became separated. Then, without warning, they were hit by (you guessed it) *another* hurricane.

Narváez's raft disappeared in the storm, tossed and turned through the churning waves, never to be seen again.

Only two of the five rafts made it to shore intact. Cabeza de Vaca woke up to his raft crashing onto the shore of an island off Galveston, Texas. Coincidentally, Dorantes and Castillo's raft washed up on the opposite side of the island. Weak and hungry, they slowly crawled onto dry land. Of the original colonists, only eighty now remained. And their problems were far from over.

As winter encroached, the shipwrecked survivors huddled around a campfire and cooked the last of their food rations. However, before they could regain their strength, they found themselves surrounded by a tribe of Native Americans once again. This time, the nomadic tribe took them in, fed them, and gave them shelter. It seemed pretty good for a minute, until it soon became apparent they were now slaves. The natives of the Texan coast were astonished by the Europeans' complete lack of fishing and hunting skills. To them, they were a bunch of lazy freeloaders, and they worked the captives really, really hard. By the following spring, less than twenty were left.

Cabeza de Vaca was eventually able to escape captivity and found another, slightly friendlier tribe in need of a neutral trader to exchange goods between warring tribes. For the next few years, Cabeza de Vaca made a living by traveling across Texas as an Indian trader. He later described many of the tribes he met by what they ate: the Roots People, the Fish People, and the Blackberry People. He learned their customs and started to understand their cultures, offering him a unique perspective that no other European had.

Then, in 1532, Cabeza de Vaca finally reunited with the last survivors of the expedition: Castillo, Dorantes, and Dorantes's African slave, Esteban the Moor. Together these four ventured off on their own. They made their way farther into the interior of North America than any other European, traveling through Texas, New Mexico, and Arizona, crisscrossing the Rio Grande. But then, just when it seemed their luck had turned around, the four survivors were captured by the Karankawa Indians. Luckily, during the next couple of years in captivity, though, Cabeza de Vaca managed to earn the respect and admiration of the tribe, becoming a medicine man and helping to heal the sick.

Finally, in 1536, Cabeza de Vaca, Dorantes, Castillo, and Esteban were discovered by a Spanish expedition in northern Mexico. It had been almost nine years since they'd first departed! The Spanish travelers were dumbfounded, completely caught off guard by Cabeza de Vaca's condition: torn clothing; a long, unkempt beard; and sun-ravaged skin.

But during his time lost in a foreign land, Álvar Núñez Cabeza de Vaca had become a new man. He ventured off in search of riches and returned a humbled soul. In nine years, he'd gone from conquistador to medicine man.

Upon returning home to Spain in 1537, Cabeza

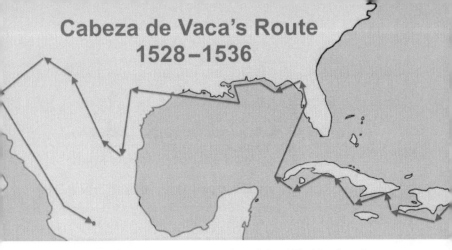

Cabeza de Vaca's Route
1528–1536

Cabeza de Vaca's amazing journey, from Cuba to Florida, along the Texas coast and through Mexico!

de Vaca dedicated the rest of his life to advocating for the rights of Native Americans and spoke out against the inhumane actions of Spanish conquistadors. Unfortunately, his tale inspired many others to foolishly set off on quests for wealth in the Americas, as he had once done. Although Cabeza de Vaca failed in his search of conquest, it seems he gained something far more valuable in his struggle for survival: compassion.

CHAPTER 7

The Seven Cities of Gold

1540–1542

*"I remained twenty-five days in this province of
Quivira . . . and what I am sure of is that there is not
any gold nor any other metal in all that country."*

—Francisco Vásquez de Coronado,
letter to the king, October 20, 1541

In September 1539, after a long journey into
the remote wilderness north of Mexico, a Franciscan monk named Marcos de Niza finally arrived at the Spanish court in Mexico City. He
was exhausted, dehydrated, and nearly dead
from his epic adventure, but he arrived at the
court of Antonio de Mendoza, the governor, with
an amazing story:

Somewhere in the wild lands north of Mexico was a massive, sprawling complex of villages, where the city gates were made of pure turquoise, the streets were paved with silver, and native kings sat on thrones of pure gold.

He told of a place called Cibola, a place better known as the Seven Cities of Gold.

If you've been paying attention to the story so far, you don't need me to tell you that this information got the Spaniards' attention.

One dude in particular, Francisco Vásquez de Coronado, was superpsyched about the idea of conquering Cibola. Coronado was born in Salamanca, Spain, in 1510 and had come to Mexico (known as "New Spain" in those days) in 1535 to make a name for himself exploring uncharted lands. Coronado worked for Mendoza for a few years and gained notoriety when he sent his army in to put down a rebellion of Native American and Black slaves who were refusing to work in the Spanish mines.

Beating up miners wasn't really the sort of glory Coronado was dreaming about when he came to the New World, so when he heard about the Seven Cities of Gold, you can imagine how excited he was to see it for himself. He volunteered to lead an expedition, promising Mendoza he would come back with more gold than any man had ever seen before in real life. Mendoza gave Coronado a ton of money for the mission, so Coronado hired 336 Spanish soldiers, had over a thousand Native American guides and porters, and bought horses, guns, armor, swords, sheep, cattle, food, and other supplies. In 1540, Francisco Vásquez de Coronado set out on an epic quest to find the legendary Cities of Gold, capture them for Spain, and return home with so much money that he'd be the most famous man in Spain.

Unfortunately for Francisco Vásquez de Coronado, the Seven Cities of Gold weren't real.

Coronado and his expedition through New Mexico to the Great Plains

When Coronado first set out, he'd been told that the lands of present-day Texas, Arizona, and New Mexico would be covered in beautiful green valleys, filled with rivers, food, and delicious animals. But after walking around for four months (which is a really long time to walk around in the desert!), all he'd found were rocks, cacti, and tribes of Native Americans who were not happy to see him.

But then, one day, off in the distance, Coronado spotted something that made his heart jump—there was a large city looming on the horizon. Most of the buildings stood between four and six stories high—a style of construction that the Spanish hadn't seen yet. This wasn't like the structures of the Aztecs or some of the other Native American tribes who had been discovered. This was something new.

Better yet, the early-morning sunlight shining on the buildings made them look as if they were a shimmering, shiny yellow. Could this be the Cities of Gold?

Nope. No they weren't. They were just white clay buildings reflecting light in a weird way. Sorry, dude.

Now, even though it wasn't made of solid gold, the Zuni Pueblo town of Hawikuh was an incredible place. The Pueblo people had mastered the art of building with a type of clay called *adobe*, and they had built a large city, with many buildings that stood taller than anything else in the region, all surrounded by a city wall. The design was so cool-looking that the Spanish would eventually adopt it, and a lot of buildings in Mexico, California, and even Florida still have a similar look. But, as you might have guessed, Francisco Vásquez de Coronado was pretty angry and disappointed that the "city of gold" was actually a city of adobe.

Coronado marched his army up to the walls, and the Zuni Pueblo came out with their weapons at the ready. They'd heard stories about how you weren't supposed to trust the Spaniards, and the Pueblo were ready for a fight.

Seething with rage at the lack of gold and at the fact that the Pueblo would dare to draw weapons against him, Coronado attacked.

Charging on his horse, his sword at the ready, Coronado led the Spanish in an attack that ripped through the Pueblo lines. Now, being attacked by a guy on a horse is such a scary thing that people were still using that strategy even in World War I, but I can only imagine that it's even more terrifying if you've never seen a horse before—and the Pueblo had never encountered horses. Most of them ran, and Coronado's soldiers forced their way through the city walls fairly easily.

The people of Hawikuh fought hard against

the invaders. They threw things from the windows of their homes down onto the Spanish; two rocks had cracked off the armored helmet of Coronado himself. A third stone hit him so hard that he had to be carried off the field of battle by his men. But, despite fighting hard, the Pueblo eventually were forced to surrender, and the Spanish took the town.

Coronado had gone searching for gold, but all he'd found in Hawikuh was a head wound. But this didn't stop him. Using Hawikuh as his base, Coronado started sending little groups of men to explore different directions, to see if maybe the Seven Cities of Gold were somewhere nearby. One of these groups found the Colorado River. Another group became the first Europeans to ever see the Grand Canyon—one of the most amazing and breathtaking geographic landmarks in North America.

Eventually Coronado moved on from Hawikuh, this time marching 180 miles to a place called Tiguex, just north of present-day Albuquerque, New Mexico. Coronado had heard rumors there was gold there, but once again he was wrong. By this point, Coronado was so enraged that he set the town on fire—every home was burned to the ground, and most of the people were killed.

By now, the indigenous people of the region had had enough of Coronado. So in the fall of 1540, a tribe told him about another city of gold. They told him about Quivira, a place where "fish are the size of horses" and everyone eats off golden plates. In reality, there was no city of gold. They just wanted him gone. Clueless, Coronado marched off again, this time up into Kansas. But there were no golden cities and horse-size goldfish to be found. By this point, Coronado wasn't doing well. His men were starving to death and openly hated him. To make matters worse, Coronado had been run over by a horse and nearly died from his injuries. Beat up, poor, hungry, and horse-stomped, Coronado decided it was time to go home.

Coronado returned to Mexico in 1542 with just a hundred men and zero gold. His three-year wild-goose chase had been a pretty Epic Fail,

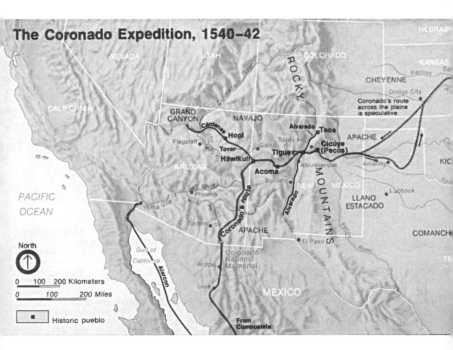

and Mendoza was very unhappy with him. Coronado was fired from his job, and because he really didn't feel like having any more adventures, he simply retired and faded into obscurity until his death in 1554.

While Coronado was considered a pretty humongous failure during his life, his expedition is actually a really important moment in American

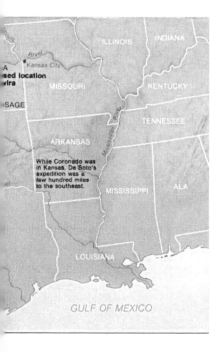

A map of Coronado's expedition through North America

history. The maps and charts he created marked the locations of the Colorado River, the Rocky Mountains, the Rio Grande, and the Grand Canyon. He was the first European to set foot in Kansas, and he was the first to see a buffalo. (Although he thought he was looking at the same "horned hairy cow with a hump" that Marco Polo wrote about in China; Marco Polo was actually looking at a yak.) Coronado and his men wrote detailed journals that tell us much about the land during this time, of the Zuni Pueblo people and customs, and they paved the way for European exploration all throughout the American Southwest.

All in all, it was a pretty incredible adventure, even if it didn't make Coronado a rich man.

CHAPTER 8
Jamestown
1606–1624

"He who does not work, will not eat."
—Captain John Smith

By the mid-sixteenth century, Spain had done a pretty excellent job of setting up well-established colonies in Mexico City, Guatemala, Santo Domingo, Peru, Florida, and a ton of other places in the New World. Hundreds of Spanish settlers were now living, working, and loading up Spanish cargo ships with gold, silver, tobacco, molasses, sugar, and other incredibly valuable things. Farther south, the Portuguese were doing well for themselves in Rio de Janeiro and other Brazilian cities. It wasn't long before the English decided they, too, wanted to set up colonies, expand their influence, and harvest everything they could from the New World. Since most of Central and South America was spoken for, the English decided that North America would be the place to go. Even though, you know, it didn't have cities of gold or silver or anything like that.

So in 1585, a dude named Sir Walter Raleigh organized expeditions to an island called Roanoke off the coast of present-day North Carolina. Raleigh brought a group of brave settlers with him; built a fort, a few houses, and a couple of farms; and soon had a half-decent colony on his hands. But when a supply ship arrived at Roanoke Island in 1587 to pick up food, medical supplies, and more colonists, there was no trace of the 115 men, women, and children who had lived there.

The once-busy village of Roanoke was now a creepy ghost town. All the homes were abandoned. There were no bodies. The only clues to be found were the word *CROATOAN* scratched into the side of an abandoned home, and the letters *CRO* carved into a tree. The supply ship's crew thought maybe this meant the settlers had moved to the nearby island of Croatoan, but when they sailed there, they found nothing. Not a trace. Four hundred and thirty years later, we still have no idea what happened to these people or where they went. It's still one of the great mysteries in American history.

The story of the Roanoke colony should give you a good idea of how incredibly brave you had to be to volunteer to be an English colonist in 1606. Facing incredible hardship, living in an unknown, brutal land, surrounded by strange people, and separated from your homeland by a once-impassable ocean, these colonists would have to depend only on their hands, brains, and guts to survive. But on December 20, 1606, 105 English men and boys boarded the ships *Susan Constant, Godspeed,* and *Discovery* and set sail to establish what would become the first permanent English settlement in America—the Jamestown colony.

In April 1607, the ships arrived off the coast of present-day Virginia. They spent two weeks scouting for a good place to build a city and finally settled on a spot along the James River that was deep enough for the ships to pull into port, yet still far enough inland that the colonists would have a bit of warning if the nearby Spanish got mad and tried to blow up their city. They named the colony Jamestown, after

England's King James I, and went to work building a town.

A couple of things made Jamestown an incredibly difficult place to live. First, the water of the James River was brackish, meaning it was half-salt and half-fresh, so you couldn't drink it or use it to water crops. Food and clean water were hard to find, disease-carrying mosquitoes were buzzing around all summer, and in the winter it got so cold that everything turned to ice and the plants would die. Oh, right, and fourteen thousand Native Americans of the Powhatan Confederacy were living in the area, and they had called  this land home since roughly 10,000 BC (give or take a few centuries). They were not excited about a bunch of Europeans building a base right in the middle of their lands without asking.

Since colonial life in North America was brutal, deadly, and unforgiving, the only way this thing was going to work was if the colonists had a leader who was as tough as the land they were trying so hard to cultivate. And they found that in Captain John Smith.

Smith was born in Lincolnshire, England, in 1580. He ran away from home at the age of sixteen, joined the Dutch Army, and fought in a huge war against the Spanish. By the age of

Captain John Smith, illustration from *The Generall Historie of Virginia, New-England and the Summer Isles*

twenty, he was in Austria, fighting for Archduke Ferdinand against the Turks, including one battle in which he single-handedly defeated three Turkish officers in a sword fight. He was wounded in a battle in Transylvania, captured by the Turks, and forced into slavery in Istanbul. But eventually he killed his master, escaped, and fought his way back to England in 1604. Since that clearly wasn't enough adventure and excitement for one lifetime, Captain Smith signed on in 1606 to take part in this new American colony, and by 1608 he was elected president of Jamestown colony.

John Smith had one main rule for his people— *no work, no food.* If you wanted to get dinner, you had to do your part in building the colony. They started harvesting lumber, making glass, and crafting pitch and tar to build roofs on their houses. Smith himself went out and mapped the area, exploring new rivers and lakes, finding places to plant crops, and trying to make peace with the Powhatan. He organized the people almost like an army, giving everyone jobs to keep the colony going. He even taught the colonists how to fight in case they were attacked by the Spanish or the Native Americans. When the first women arrived at Jamestown in 1608, he found jobs for them as well, to ensure that everyone contributed in keeping the colony alive.

Things got a little dicey, however, when Smith went out to explore one day and was ambushed by a group of Powhatan warriors. They took Smith to see the chief of the Powhatan, Wahunsenacawh, who demanded to know what was going on with all this European colony nonsense. Smith tried to act tough, but Wahunsenacawh wasn't buying it. He sentenced Smith to death and ordered one of his warriors to chop off the Englishman's head.

Then, according to an account later written by John Smith, at the last minute, Wahunsenacawh's daughter, a ten-year-old girl named Pocahontas, stepped in and begged her father not to kill him. Her dad agreed and let Smith go. A few months later, Wahunsenacawh even sent a large shipment of food to the colonists to help them during the difficult winter. It's likely that Jamestown

An 1870 depiction of Pocahontas rescuing John Smith from her tribe, considered to be highly inaccurate

would have perished without the Powhatan chief's intervention.

In September 1609, Captain Smith was injured

when a big stock of gunpowder blew up in his face and burned him badly. He went back home to England to recover, and Jamestown felt his loss immediately. The winter after his departure is called the "starving time," which is just as bad as it sounds. Crops died. The English and the Powhatan fought constantly. Colonists were being killed in battle, starving to death, or dying of disease. Things were getting really, really bad, and if help didn't arrive soon, the colony was going to go extinct.

Before sailing for England, John Smith had written a strongly worded letter, which is now known (awesomely) as "Smith's Rude Answer," in which he basically demanded that England send him more men and supplies so that Jamestown didn't completely fall apart. His call was answered in June 1609, when the three-hundred-ton merchant ship *Sea Venture* left for Virginia carrying a huge shipment of food, supplies, and experienced carpenters, laborers, masons, and other workers.

Of course, because nothing has ever gone exactly according to plan in the history of the world, the *Sea Venture* got caught in a hurricane that slammed the ship for four days and nights. The ship was so badly damaged that Captain Christopher Newport (a big, giant dude with a huge beard, who had commanded the first expedition that landed at Jamestown) was forced to beach the ship on an uninhabited island we know today as Bermuda.

By the time the *Sea Venture* crew built a new ship and sailed into Jamestown harbor, almost a year later, only sixty colonists were left alive. The town walls and buildings were wrecked and in shambles. The colonists were hungry and half-dead, and many of them were considering abandoning the colony. The arrival of Newport and his crew brought new life to Jamestown. Another man, a farmer named John Rolfe, is also responsible for revitalizing the colony: He figured out a way to grow tobacco right there in Jamestown—a crop most had assumed was capable of being grown only in the southern colonies controlled by Spain.

Now, okay, cigarettes and smoking are bad for you. You should never do this. We all know that. But, in 1616, nobody knew what cancer was, and nobody really knew that tobacco was super-bad for you, so pretty much everybody did it. And since tobacco didn't grow anywhere in England, when Rolfe started growing it successfully in Virginia, he immediately made Jamestown a *ton* of money. The colony was saved, Rolfe eventually married Pocahontas to make peace between the settlers and the Powhatan, and in 1624, Virginia became an official royal colony with Jamestown as its capital. Jamestown would remain the capital of Virginia until 1699, a year

The *Mayflower* in Plymouth Harbor

after a big fire destroyed the government build-ing, and the capital was moved to Williamsburg. If you visit Williamsburg, Virginia, today, you can still see some of the original buildings dat-ing back to roughly this time!

Another famous colony that sprang up not long after Jamestown was Plymouth colony, in what is now Massachusetts. Plymouth was set-tled by a group of pilgrims in 1620, who arrived aboard the *Mayflower*. The pilgrims had a rough time during their first winter in America, but were aided by Squanto, a member of the Patuxet tribe. Together, the pilgrims and the local Native Americans of the Wampanoag tribe celebrated their first harvest with a feast, known today as "the First Thanksgiving."

In a lot of ways, Jamestown and Plymouth were the beginning of what would later become the United States of America, which started as just thirteen colonies and eventually grew to fifty states, stretching from coast to coast. The American frontier would remain mostly unexplored until 1804 with the Lewis and Clark expedition, sent out by President Thomas Jefferson.

A somewhat inaccurate depiction of the First Thanksgiving, between the Pilgrims and natives at Plymouth

CHAPTER 9

Captain Cook's Last Voyage

1768–1779

"Hardly anything works out as well as we hope."

—James Cook

James Cook was one of the greatest explorers of the eighteenth century. He made three voyages across the Pacific Ocean, mapped both Australia and New Zealand, and was the first European to discover Hawaii. But perhaps his greatest achievement was curing scurvy!

Captain Cook (not to be confused with Captain Hook) was a British commander in the

Captain James Cook

Royal Navy. Cook was a master navigator and cartographer. In 1766, after serving in the Seven Years War, he was given his first command: HMS *Endeavour.*

By the eighteenth century, the British Empire was the most powerful empire on the planet, with colonies spanning from India to North

America and the largest fleet of ships ever built. But there were still uncharted waters and new lands and wealth waiting to be discovered. To Europeans, the great unknown was the vast Pacific Ocean.

Lieutenant Cook set out on his first voyage in 1768. The *Endeavour* was on a mission to transport a group of English astronomers to Tahiti (a small island in the Pacific) to observe the planet Venus as it passed in front of the sun in June 1769. They sailed across the Atlantic, rounded Cape Horn at the tip of South America, and continued westward, arriving at the tropical island with a couple of months to spare. After dropping passengers in Tahiti, Cook and his crew ventured southwest toward New Zealand—a group of islands previously visited by Dutch explorer Abel Tasman—who, on his first voyage, sailed all around the perimeter of Australia without realizing he'd missed the continent completely!

During his time in New
Zealand, Cook claimed
both islands for Great
Britain and was the
first to (accurately)
chart its thousands
of miles of coast-

line. Next, they sailed up the east coast of
Australia and claimed this new landmass as
New South Wales. It was there that Cook made
landfall at a place he named *Botany Bay*—
after all the unique plant specimens his botanists
collected—and met a tribe of aboriginal natives.
Upon his return home, Cook was promoted to
commander.

One of Cook's greatest accomplishments was
in successfully remedying scurvy on his long
multiyear voyages around the world. This was
thanks to his attention to hygiene and a healthy,
vitamin-rich diet, for both himself and his crew.

Scurvy was a dreaded disease; it had claimed more lives than any other seafaring hazard. Back home, Cook became an overnight celebrity thanks to his published journals and scientific exploits from around the world.

Later, in 1772, Cook shipped off for his second voyage aboard HMS *Resolution*, along with HMS *Adventure*. This time, Cook set out in search of the fabled "Southern Continent." For centuries, many believed there was another, yet undiscovered, continent at Earth's southernmost tip. This idea wasn't based on any real knowledge of its existence—but rather just a theory that the landmass of the Northern Hemisphere would be balanced by a landmass of equal size in the Southern Hemisphere. Though no one had ever laid eyes on this Southern Continent, it was often printed on world maps. Cook tried to sail into the icy southern waters twice,

but he was forced to turn back for warmer waters both times— never realizing they were just off the coast of Antarctica. Ironically, it was Cook's failed expeditions that caused cartographers to remove the fabled Southern Continent from their maps. It would be almost another fifty years before another explorer confirmed the existence of Antarctica.

In 1776, Captain James Cook set sail on his third and final voyage—on a quest to find that same (nonexistent) Northwest Passage. Cook once again commanded HMS *Resolution*, which was joined by HMS *Discovery*. This time, Cook sailed east, around the Cape of Good Hope in Africa, across the Indian Ocean, and through

New Zealand. He made a pit stop in Tahiti before heading northeast through the heart of the Pacific Ocean.

In January 1778, they spotted land in the distance. It was a chain of volcanic islands we now know as Hawaii. Instead, Cook called them the "Sandwich Islands," which he named after the Earl of Sandwich, John Montagu—who sponsored Cook's voyages. The crews of the

The HMS *Resolution* and *Discovery* in Tahiti

Resolution and *Discovery* may have been the first Europeans to set foot on the beaches of Hawaii, but the islands were home to at least 250,000 Polynesians who had settled the islands over a thousand years earlier. The native islanders were, at first, welcoming of the fair-skinned explorers and were curious about their ships and iron.

After trading supplies, the *Resolution* and *Discovery* continued their journey north to find a passage around North America to the Atlantic. They soon realized, like all the explorers before them, that the Northwest Passage didn't exist, so they eventually gave up and turned back from the freezing waters of the Bering Strait (named after Danish explorer Vitus Bering). Along the way, though, Cook managed to map most of the northwest North American coast, including Alaska. The ships sailed back to Hawaii, this time docking in Kealakekua Bay, the sacred harbor of the Hawaiian fertility god Lono. Their arrival just so happened to coincide with the festival of Lono, and the Hawaiians saw this as a sign and treated the Europeans like gods. King Kalaniopuu lavished his honored guests with gifts.

When one of Cook's crew members later died, they were exposed as mere mortals. After they had exploited the natives' goodwill, relations with the Hawaiians became further strained. After realizing they were no longer welcome, Captain Cook shipped out on February 4, 1779. As fate would have it, Cook's ship was damaged in rough seas, forcing them to return once again to Hawaii. This time, things went much less smoothly.

Captain Cook and his crew went to the natives for help repairing their ship, but they were instead met with hurled rocks. While they were moored one night, a group of Hawaiians stole

one of Cook's smaller boats, and at one point, during a scuffle, one of the crew members shot King Kalaniopuu's nephew. Cook decided to take matters into his own hands and tried to kidnap and ransom the king for his stolen boat. While Cook was dragging King Kalaniopuu toward the beach, a fight broke out. During the battle, Captain James Cook was struck in the

A stylized depiction of the death of Captain Cook at the hands of Hawaiian natives

back of the head by a club. As he fell, he was killed by the thrust of a spear.

The Hawaiians, who respected Cook despite their falling out, gave him proper Hawaiian burial rites that were usually reserved for only high elders and chiefs. As a sign of truce, King Kalaniopuu returned (most of) Cook's remains to his crew for a formal burial at sea.

Despite his grisly end, Captain Cook is still considered one of the last great voyagers of the Age of Exploration. By charting the Pacific Ocean, Cook helped to give us a clearer picture of the wider world. His scientific accomplishments helped advance our understanding of nature, and, more important, his breakthrough in combating scurvy saved countless lives for many years to come.

CHAPTER 10
Dr. Livingstone and the Quest for the Nile
1871

"Dr. Livingstone, I presume?"

—Sir Henry Morton Stanley

D*r. *David Livingstone was a remarkable and complicated man. He was an intrepid explorer, medical doctor, writer, Protestant missionary, scientific investigator, and passionate antislavery advocate. Dr. Livingstone was the first European to journey into the heart of Africa, making it his life's goal to find the source of the Nile—not for riches or glory, but because he believed that by doing so, he could open the continent to the rest of the world and end the African slave trade once and for all.

Livingstone grew up in Scotland in the early nineteenth century, where he used the money he earned from working at a factory to buy books to educate himself on science, theology, and geography. In 1839, while he was still studying medicine in London, Livingstone met Robert Moffat, a missionary from South Africa, and was introduced to Sir Thomas Fowell Buxton. Buxton was a British abolitionist who strongly felt that the slave trade could be eliminated through legitimate trade and the spread of Christianity. Inspired by these men, on November 20, 1840, David Livingstone was ordained as a missionary and immediately set sail for South Africa, arriving in Cape Town on March 14, 1841.

At the time, much of Africa was a mystery to the outside world. In the fourteenth century,

David Livingstone

Ibn Battuta was a Moroccan scholar and traveler who explored the far reaches of the Muslim world.

famous Moroccan scholar Ibn Battuta explored from China to as far as West Africa by land, and renowned Portuguese explorer Vasco da Gama explored the east coast of Africa by sea in 1497, but few Europeans after that had ventured into the heart of Africa and even fewer had returned. The courageous Dr. Livingstone was undeterred.

As a die-hard abolitionist, Livingstone hated slavery and was passionate about bringing awareness to the world. He had hoped that exploring the continent would open roads for trade, commerce, and civilization, ultimately ending the slave trade in Africa.

During one of his early mission trips into uncharted territory, Livingstone was mauled by a lion! Miraculously, he survived the encounter with nothing more than a wounded arm. Despite the injury, the brave Livingstone pushed on farther north, once saying, "I shall open up a path into the interior or perish."

In 1845, he married Robert Moffat's daughter, Mary, who accompanied him on his journeys until she was forced to return to Scotland with their children because of health complications. Livingstone spent the next decade exploring the African interior and meeting native African tribes along the way. To spread commerce and goodwill, Livingstone became the first European to cross the continent by foot.

A drawing of the Zulu tribe from Dr. Livingstone's *Narrative of an Expedition to the Zambesi and its Tributaries*

He traveled up the Linyanti River in Angola on Africa's west coast to Shupanga in Mozambique. Two of Livingstone's biggest advantages were that he traveled light and didn't travel with a large contingent of heavily armed men, which made him more approachable to the locals and less of a threat. During his quest, he encountered the Zulu tribe, discovered Lake Ngami and what he named Victoria Falls, on the Zambezi River on the border of Zambia and Zimbabwe.

Livingstone became an overnight sensation upon his return to England, and his first book, *Missionary Travels and Researches in South Africa*, quickly sold seventy thousand copies! David Livingstone geared up for a second expedition in 1858, this time joined by a team, with the goal of setting up a British missionary settlement in Africa. The group immediately ran into problem after problem, eventually forcing the British government to recall the expedition.

After a quick detour to India, Livingstone made his way back to England in 1864. Although

his second journey to Africa was at first seen as a complete bust, it had in fact amassed an invaluable amount of scientific research in the region—and more important, Livingstone was bringing more awareness to the plight of the African people from the evils of the transatlantic slave trade. Livingstone did not give up easily: "I am prepared to go anywhere, provided it be forward."

Dr. Livingstone decided his next goal would be to locate the source of the Nile. The Nile is a river in Africa that runs north, up through Egypt, and back in the day, Europeans had no idea how big the Nile was or even where it began. At the time, many believed that the river's source was Victoria Falls, the waterfall that Livingstone had first come across in his early expeditions, but Livingstone wasn't convinced. For this occasion, he assembled a group of Asian and African guides to assist him on his journey. On

January 28, 1866, Livingstone arrived in Zanzibar, on the east coast, and began his trek at the foot of the Ruvuma River.

Unfortunately, the expedition took a turn for the worse when, tired of the backbreaking and perilous journey, Livingstone's men started to desert him. Some of the deserters even falsely claimed that Livingstone had been killed by the Ngoni tribe. The more tirelessly he pushed forward, the more his men abandoned him. One of his former companions even stole his medical chest! Despite all these setbacks, Livingstone pressed on, continuing west, more determined than ever.

Eventually, Dr. Livingstone was joined by some Arab traders, who helped him reach Tanganyika, part of modern-day Tanzania, in February 1869. From there, he continued west and became the first European to reach Lake Mweru, on the border of the Congo, and then Lake

Bangweulu, in the heart of Zambia. It was then that Livingstone fell desperately ill, trudging through bacteria-laden swamplands without any medical supplies. He made it to the source of the Congo River and was forced to turn back instead of venturing farther into the rain forest. His health was in rapid decline, and he had been missing for years to the outside world. Many had presumed him a goner.

Then, on November 10, 1871, a correspondent for the *New York Herald*, Henry Morton Stanley, walked into the African village of Ujiji and spotted a pale man with a gray beard. Stanley waved and raised his hat at the older man. "Dr. Livingstone, I presume?" he said jokingly.

Livingstone responded with, "Yes ... I feel thankful that I am here to welcome you." At the time, David Livingstone had been missing for

An illustrated depiction of the famous meeting between Sir Henry Morton Stanley and Dr. David Livingstone, from Stanley's book *How I Found Livingstone*

six years and was no closer to finding the source of the Nile. Stanley urged Livingstone to come back with him to London, but Livingstone insisted on continuing his quest for the Nile.

Dr. Livingstone ventured on, heading farther south (in the opposite direction of the Nile), eventually making his way to Chief Chitambo's village, where he succumbed to malaria in 1873 and died at the age of sixty. His African companions performed a traditional ritual, burying his heart under a baobab tree. In 1874, a ship carried Livingstone's body and journal back to England, where he was buried at Westminster Abbey. Livingstone may not have found the source of the Nile, but what he helped to achieve was a far greater accomplishment: the abolition of slavery.

Unfortunately, his writings and expeditions also had the unintended consequence of paving the way for colonialism. Countries scrambled to carve up Africa for its riches, with little thought to the rich cultures that resided there, which eventually destabilized the entire region. Livingstone's legacy is another reminder of the wonders and perils of globalization.

The world has changed so much in such a short period of time that it's hard to imagine what it was like to live in an era where most of the earth was still mystery. Today the world is more interconnected than ever before. Thanks to technology, we've become a global society. A person from New York can chat with a friend in Hong Kong as if they were in the same room, despite being eight thousand miles and twelve time zones away! None of that would be possi-ble today if it wasn't for the pioneering spirit of explorers like

Columbus, Cabeza de Vaca, and Dr. David Livingstone.

While these men achieved some amazing things, many of their discoveries are also responsible for many not-so-great things, like the extinction of animal species, the loss of irreplaceable cultures, and the spread of deadly diseases like measles and smallpox, which wiped out entire populations of native peoples—a stark reminder that scientific discovery must always be coupled with empathy, caution, and diligent awareness.

From Leif Erikson's discovery of America to Marco Polo's journey across Asia to Magellan's groundbreaking circumnavigation of the globe and beyond, history is chock-full of brave explorers, incredible men and women constantly pushing the boundaries of the unknown. The great Age of Exploration may be over, but the human spirit of adventure lives on. Despite all that's been uncovered, humankind has only begun to scratch the surface: uncharted mysteries still lie beneath the seas, deep in the jungles, and far beyond the stars—waiting to be discovered . . .

TIMELINE

1000   Leif Erikson becomes the first European to discover North America

1271   Marco Polo joins his family on a journey to China

1295   Marco Polo returns home to Italy

1405   Chinese Fleet Admiral Zheng-He departs on his first of seven voyages

1492   Christopher Columbus embarks on his historic voyage across the Atlantic

1500   Columbus is arrested and sent back to Spain

1507   The Americas are officially given their name, after navigator and cartographer Amerigo Vespucci

1513   Ponce de Leon's expedition to Florida

1518   Spanish conquistador Hernando Cortés begins his conquest of the Aztec Empire in Mexico

1519   Ferdinand Magellan embarks on his three-year journey around the globe

1521   Magellan dies before reaching the end of his ground-breaking voyage

1524   Giovanni da Verrazzano's voyage up the eastern coast of North America to New York in search of the Northwest Passage to the Pacific Ocean

1527 Cabeza de Vaca sets out on Narváez's doomed conquest of Florida

1536 Cabeza de Vaca and three other survivors of the derailed expedition are found wandering around Mexico

1540 Francisco Vásquez de Coronado begins his quest for the fabled Seven Cities of Gold in the North American Southwest

1585 "The Lost Colony of Roanoke" is first founded

1607 The first (permanent) British settlement is established in America: the colony of Jamestown (Virginia)

1621 The *Mayflower* arrives at Plymouth Rock (Massachusetts), where the Pilgrims celebrate "the First Thanksgiving" with the Wampanoag tribe

1768 Captain James Cook sets sail on his first epic voyage, aboard HMS *Endeavour*

1779 Captain Cook meets his end in Hawaii

1804 The Lewis and Clark expedition sets out across the North American frontier

1841 Dr. David Livingstone arrives in Cape Town, South Africa, on his first expedition into the heart of the continent

1871 Henry Morton Stanley finds Dr. Livingstone in Africa, after he went missing six years earlier in his search for the source of the Nile

ACKNOWLEDGMENTS

The authors would like to thank our amazing editors, Simon Boughton and Connie Hsu, for believing in this project and giving us the opportunity to write it, and to our agent, Farley Chase of Chase Literary, for helping us work out all the details to make this happen. Thanks also to our editor, Mekisha Telfer, and our copy editors, Sally Doherty and Tracy Koontz, for their excellent work helping us get this book into shape. And, most of all, we would like to thank you, the reader, for taking the time to read this book! Without your support, none of this could be possible. We really hope you liked it.

Erik would like to first thank Ben for the amazing opportunity to work on this project—it really is a dream come true. I, of course, want to acknowledge all my friends and family for their support over the years, as well as anyone and everyone who has ever encouraged me to keep on writing.

A very special shout-out to: David Kowalski (for helping to brainstorm the concept of writing about historical failures), Chris Carroll (for introducing me to blogging), Justin Ache (for helping me redesign my website and hosting it), James Lester (for inspiring me to keep the history blog going), Neil Sindicich (for giving me the opportunity to build up my online writing portfolio), Max Michaels (for my first writing gig in print), Damian Fox (for pushing me to pursue publication and helping me put together my first pitch), John Wesley Moody (my college history professor), Jason Whitmarsh (my humanities professor), my Patreon patrons, who have financially supported my blogging habit over the years, and to Dani Slader—who put up with me every step of the way. Finally, I want to thank Meg—for her endless support and love during the craziest year of my life.

(If I missed anyone, it's only because I'm already way over my word count.)

Ben would like to say a very special thank-you to the wonderful and lovely Thaís Melo, for being my inspiration, my muse, and the most incredible woman that any man could ever ask for. You make me so unbelievably happy, and without your constant love, support, and encouragement, none of this could have been possible. This book (or at least my half of it) is dedicated to you.

BIBLIOGRAPHY

Cool Websites

britannica.com

historicjamestowne.org

history.com

historyisfun.org

nationalgeographic.com

nps.gov

pbs.org

Books

Ambrose, Stephen E. *Undaunted Courage.* New York: Simon & Schuster, 1996.

Benge, Janet, and Geoff Benge. *Captain John Smith: A Foothold in the New World.* Lynnwood, WA: Emerald Books, 2006.

Ciment, James. *Colonial America.* New York: Routledge, 2006.

Coronado, Francisco Vásquez de, and Pedro Reyes Castañeda. *The Journey of Coronado.* Trans. George Parker Winship. New York: A.S. Barnes and Co., 1904.

Eirik the Red and Other Icelandic Sagas. Trans. Gwyn Jones. New York: Oxford University Press, 1999.

Favor, Lesli J. *Francisco Vásquez de Coronado.* New York: Rosen Publishing, 2003.

Fifer, Barbara. *Going Along with Lewis & Clark.* Helena, MT: Montana Magazine, 2000.

Fleming, Fergus. *Off the Map: Tales of Endurance and Exploration*. New York: Grove Press, 2004.

Gitlin, Martin. *Giovanni da Verrazzano: Explorer of the Atlantic Coast of North America*. New York: Rosen Publishing, 2016.

Hazen, Walter A. *Explorers of the New World, Grades 4–7*. Quincy, IL: Mark Twain Media, 1994.

Heat-Moon, William Least. *Columbus in the Americas*. Hoboken, NJ: Wiley, 2002.

Jones, Gwyn. *A History of the Vikings*. London: Oxford University Press, 2001.

Lewis, Meriwether, and William Clark. *The Journals of Lewis and Clark*. Washington, DC: National Geographic, 2002.

Mancall, Peter C. *Fatal Journey*. New York: Basic Books, 2009.

Mann, Charles C. *1491*. New York: Knopf, 2005.

Matthews, Rupert. *Eyewitness: Explorer*. New York: Dorling Kindersley, 2012.

Mattox, Jake, ed. *Explorers of the New World*. San Diego, CA: Greenhaven Press, 2003.

McCudden, Mary Rose. *Britannica Student Encyclopedia*. Chicago: Encyclopedia Britannica, 2015.

Mountjoy, Shane. *Francisco Coronado and the Seven Cities of Gold*. Ed. William H. Goetzmann. Philadelphia: Chelsea House, 2006.

Oliver, James A. *The Bering Strait Crossing*. Exmouth, UK: Information Architects, 2006.

Philbrick, Nathaniel. *Mayflower*. New York: Viking, 2006.

Pierce, Alan. *The Jamestown Colony*. Edina, MN: Abdo Publishing, 2004.

Proulx, Gilles. *Between France and New France: Life Aboard the Tall Sailing Ships*. Toronto: Dundurn Press, 2008.

Resendez, Andres. *A Land So Strange: The Epic Journey of Cabeza de Vaca*. New York: Basic Books, 2007.

Rodger, Ellen. *Lewis and Clark: Opening the American West*. St. Catharines, ON: Crabtree Publishing, 2005.

Roesdahl, Else. *The Vikings*. London: Penguin, 1987.

Sansevere-Dreher, Diane. *Explorers Who Got Lost*. New York: Starscape, 1992.

Smith, John. *The Journals of Captain John Smith*. Ed. John Thompson. Washington, DC: National Geographic, 2007.

Tucker, Spencer C., James Arnold, and Roberta Wiener, eds. *The Encyclopedia of the North American Indian Wars, 1607–1890*. Santa Barbara, CA: ABC-CLIO, 2011.

Wiesner-Hanks, Merry E. *An Age of Voyages, 1350–1600*. New York: Oxford University Press, 2005.

Wulffson, Don. *Before Columbus: Early Voyages to the Americas*. Minneapolis, MN: Twenty-First Century Books, 2008.

INDEX

Number in **bold** indicate pages with illustrations

PICTURE CREDITS